Remains To Be Seen

By Lee Mueller

©1998

Caution: Professionals and amateurs are hereby advised that REMAINS TO BE SEEN is subject to a royalty. It is fully protected under the copyright laws of the United States of America and of all countries covered by International
Copyright union (including the Dominion of Canada and the rest of the British Commonwealth) and of all countries covered by the Pan-American Copyright Convention and the Universal Copyright, and of all countries with which the United States has reciprocal copyright relations. All rights including professional, amateur, motion picture, recitation, lecturing, public reading,radio broadcasting,television,video or sound taping, all other forms of mechanical or electronic reproduction, such as information storage and retrieval systems and photocopying, and the rights of translation into foreign languages, are strictly reserved. All inquiries concerning rights should be addressed to Playedwell,LLC - play-dead.com.

Characters

Bud and Mac* - two janitors of "U Do It" Trunk Rental Company

Narrator- Moves the plot along.

Sam* and Ella- proprietors of the U Do It store in local town.

Officers Badman and Goodman- two local police officers who start and assist in the investigation.

Agents Muledeer and Sullen- two FBI agents who take up the investigation.

Iggy and Trixie – shady characters in a local tavern

George and Martha- proprietors of the U Do It office in another city.

Madame DuBoys- a washed up old time film star waiting for the elusive close up

Noel- Madame's inebriated personal assistant

Edie Buffet and Nick Niagra- a couple of lack luster lounge singers.

Set is plain since it will represent various locations. In original production the "trunk" was used as a set piece in different scenes – e.g. to represent a counter, a table.. etc...

MAC walks onto stage sweeping floor- walks around for a few beats.

BUD: (*from just off stage*) Hey Mac!

MAC: Yea Bud?

BUD: Somebody left a trunk in one of these rentals.

MAC: A what?

BUD: A trunk.

MAC: Left it where?

BUD: In one the trucks.

MAC: A trunk?

BUD: Yea, in a truck.

MAC: Left a trunk in a truck?

BUD: Yea. I guess when they left the truck, they left the trunk. What should we do with it?

MAC: Leave it in lost and found, I guess.

BUD: O.K. Could you give me hand, it's kinda heavy.

MAC: What do I look like? A heavy lifting... lifter of heavy things?

BUD: Well, actually.. yea, kinda.

MAC: Really? O.K. Cool

BUD and MAC pull a large steamer trunk up onto stage center. -Ad lib through this action. "Watch it - it's heavy etc.."

MAC: Did you check it out?

BUD: Who me? Naw. Wonder what's in it?

MAC: Why don't you check it out?

BUD: Who me? Naw.

Both look down at it for a moment, then..

BUD: O.K.! Let's look.

MAC: Yea, O.K.

They struggle with lock for a minute.

MAC: I think it's locked Bud.

BUD: Yea. I think you're right.

MAC: *(beat)* You gotta Bobbie Pin?

BUD: Why would I have a Bobbie Pin? Do I look like Bobbie Pin people?

MAC: No, I guess you're really not a Bobbie type. More in the safety pin realm. *(beat)* You gotta safety pin?

BUD: Nope.

MAC: A needle'?

BUD: Nope.

MAC: Ice pick? A small allen wrench? (*BUD shakes his head at each*) A finishing nail? Needle nose pliers? Wire cutters? Swiss Army Knife? A cork screw? Tweezers?

BUD: Nope.

MAC: A small two gauge rotary de-fragmenting reverse polarity pine lock-picker?

BUD: Yea. (*takes toothpick from mouth -hands it to max*) Here ya go.

MAC: Thanks. (*bends down -quickly picks lock - and opens trunk*) You see what I see Bud?

BUD: I think so. You smell what I smell?

MAC: Oh yea. Big time.

   (*Both wave hand in front of faces*)

BUD: Is "that" what it looks like?

MAC: It looks like it. You think we should we tell somebody?

BUD: I don't know Mac. Do you want to tell somebody that we saw some...body? They'll ask us questions, they'll check our backgrounds, it'll be a big long ordeal. Days. Maybe months. We'll miss work, our families, our favorite prime time programs. You wanna tell somebody?

MAC: Who me? Naw!

BUD: So, did we "see" something?

MAC: Nope. I didn't see nothing resembling something. Did you?

BUD: In where?

MAC: Exactly. Nothin' was seen. (*shuts trunk lid*)

BUD: Nothin' was smelled.

MAC: I really gotta be going, Bud.

BUD: Yea, we best be going.

MAC: Yea. Let's go.

BUD: You need a lift home?

MAC: No, I'm gunna wait.

BUD: Wait for who?

MAC: Goddot.

BUD: What an obscure reference my friend.

They remain frozen on stage as Narrator enters.

NARRATOR: Good evening. Presented for your permission. Submitted for your acceptance. From a place where mystery and intrigue loom just out of reach, like so many carrots dangled before the horses, we turn our attention to something more accessible. Where the carrots are not dangled as far and the horses are faster. Where time and space are roommates and take turns doing the dishes. Where approval is the sound of one hand clapping. Where matter and energy are distant cousins. You're crossing over into a dimension that's a short walk on a long pier. Next signpost up ahead.... "Fine for littering."

(*BUD and max exit as Sam and Ella enter scene carrying clipboards -ELLA goes to trunk -SAM goes stage right as if checking of items from list*)

NARRATOR: (*cont.*) Proposed for your approval. Tonight, we find ourselves at the final resting place of what appears to be an ordinary trunk. In fact, it doesn't appear to be an ordinary trunk, it *is* an ordinary trunk. A trunk that has found its way to this location, the "You Do It" Truck Rental Company. Where did the trunk come from?

ELLA: Where did this trunk come from?

NARRATOR: Where is it going? Where has it been?

SAM: What trunk?

NARRATOR: All these questions and more can only be answered, once we visit that distant realm, that far off point just left of center... or from where you're sitting.. it would be your right... that mysterious complex nebula called.... the Mystery Zone.

(*ELLA opens up trunk and gasps- waves hand from odor*)

ELLA: Sam? Sam somebody's here.

SAM: (*with back to her*) I'll be with 'em in just in minute.

ELLA: No Sam, I mean... they're here! (*pointing into trunk*)

SAM: Really? (*turns around as if to greet someone*) Welcome to You Do It - Truck Rental, we offer discount rates.... (*looking around*) uh... Ella? I thought you said there was somebody here?

ELLA: No! In here! There's somebody in here!

SAM: In where?

ELLA: In here. This trunk.

SAM: Well, what are they doing in there? (*crosses to trunk*)

ELLA: Not very much. Certainly not moving or breathing. Death can limit you.

SAM: Oh my. Oh dear. Oh boy.

ELLA: We'd better call someone.

SAM: Oh yes. We'd better call someone.

ELLA: Why don't you call Sam?

SAM: Why don't you?

ELLA: No, you do it.

SAM: No, you do it!

ELLA: Sam!

SAM: All right. I'll do it. (*beat*) Who should I call?

ELLA: We'd better call an ambulance!

SAM: Yes, good idea. (*starts to cross away*) Uh...wait. I believe one calls an ambulance when someone is injured. That fellow may have been injured at some point, but now an ambulance is beside the point.

ELLA: Who do you suggest we call?

SAM: Just an educated guess but I would say a hearse is in order. But I don't suppose one can just call a hearse.

ELLA: Why don't you just call 911 and let them wrestle with the problem.

SAM: Very well. (*turns his back -mimes phone call*)

ELLA: No telling where this person came from. I suppose we could check the records and see which truck it came from. Maybe the last person who rented it accidentally left it there. Most people leave "bungee cords" and "coat hangers" on the trucks-- occasionally they might leave a shoe or other various sundry items, but nobody's ever left a trunk with a body in it. Although there was that one couple who left their grandmother in the truck. Remember that Sam? Poor thing was in there over the entire Thanksgiving weekend before we found her. Thankfully, she had a purse full of dinner crackers and a bottle of Maalox, otherwise she never would've made it.

SAM: (*on phone*) Yes, hello? This is the You Do It Truck Rental Company, we have a body in a trunk. No, in a trunk. But it came off a truck. (*beat*) Yes, the trunk was on a truck. (*beat*) Yes, the body's in a trunk and the trunk was a on truck. That's correct.

Detective GOODMAN and Inspector BADHAM enter in back - they begin dialogue as they make their way through audience toward the stage. Badham is finishing a do-nut and a large cup of coffee.

NARRATOR: Detective Goodman and Inspector Badham received the call at 8:15 and made all haste to designated location. The You Do It Truck rental company. They learned that the proprietors, a Mr Sam and Eleanor G. Frinkle had discovered a body in a trunk on their premises. What these two police officers were about to walk into, was more twisted than any double glazed donut confection. One of the most sorted cases from the Mystery zone files. Would hope be lost? Or only the policemen?

BADHAM: Hold on, hold on! I thought they said it was a left after the gas station!

(*They both stop and play this out half way to stage*)

GOODMAN: Uh.. yes. I believe that to be correct.

BADHAM : Didn't we make a right?

GOODMAN: I believe we made a left.

BADHAM : You sure?

GOODMAN: I'm reasonably certain we are on the correct street.

BADHAM : You're reasonably certain?

GOODMAN: Yes. I am 99.9 percent sure.

BADHAM : How do you know? How do you know your certainty is that reasonable? What reason should I have that your certain? Huh? How can I be certain that you're certain? What reasons do you have to be so certain?

GOODMAN: *(points to stage)* Because it's right there. The You Do It truck rental.

BADHAM : Oh yea. That's a pretty good reason.

   Detectives go up onto stage.

GOODMAN: Mr. and Mrs. Frinkle? I'm Detective Goodman and this is Inspector Badham.

ELLA: Please call me Ella.

SAM: Call me Sam.

BADHAM : Sam and Ella?

GOODMAN: Very well. We understand you found a body in a trunk.

ELLA: Yes, that trunk right there.

   BADHAM goes to it and opens it.

BADHAM : *(reacts to smell)* Wheeeeew!!! Holy Guacamole!

ELLA: Someone left it on one of our rental trucks.

BADHAM: I'd say this body's been in here for quite a while.

GOODMAN: Do you have any idea, which truck the *trunk* came from?

SAM: I checked the ledger and there was only one truck returned last night.

GOODMAN: Could I see the ledger?

SAM: Sure. (*crosses away*)

BADHAM: How'd the trunk get in here? Did someone haul it in?

ELLA: I'm assuming the workers did.

GOODMAN: Workers?

ELLA: Yes. We have a couple of workers that handle the rentals when they come back. You know, check the oil, wiper fluid and stuff. If they find anything left on the trucks, they haul it in here.

BADHAM: Are these workers here now?

ELLA: No, they work after hours.

BADHAM: Graveyard shift?

ELLA: Yes. Some people call it that. They'll be here tonight if you need to ask them anything.

SAM: (*coming back with ledger*) Here you go Detective. It's Rental Trunk number 9.

GOODMAN: (*looking at page*) I see.

BADHAM : (*looking over Goodman's shoulder*) So, this is a list of all the people who have rented the truck? And these would be their current addresses and phone numbers?

SAM: Yep. That's all of 'em.

GOODMAN: I see.

BADHAM: So all we need to do is go to the last person who rented the truck and see what they know about the trunk with the dead body.

GOODMAN: I. C.

BADHAM: Potentially that could be our perpetrator and case closed. Depending on who the last person was, that rented it.

GOODMAN: I.C.

BADHAM: What do you think Goodman ?

GOODMAN: I.C.

BADHAM: I know "you see", I'm asking you, what do you think?

GOODMAN: No, I. C. The initials of the last person who rented it. I.C.

BADHAM: Oh, I see.

GOODMAN: Only used initials, Not a full name. But we have the address here.

BADHAM: Do either of you remember an I.C. ?

SAM: Can't say that I do.

ELLA: No. I've known some cool people, but no one who's I.C.

SAM: Ha. That's a good one there Ella.

BADHAM: This ain't no joking matter Vanilla Ice! You have a dead body in a trunk here and it's on your premises. Now I suggest you get on your mental running suit and jog your memory.

ELLA: Honest, I don't remember! Trunks come in and out of here all the time.

GOODMAN: I see here where they rented truck number 9. It originated in (nearby city) And was returned here.

BADHAM: (*nearby city*)? It came from (*nearby city*) ?

SAM: Oh yes, we have franchises all over. You can rent our trucks in almost any city and return them in any city.

BADHAM: So, this trunk could've come from anywhere? Any number of cities?

SAM: Anywhere.

ELLA: Anyplace.

GOODMAN: Anytime.

BADHAM: Any ideas?

GOODMAN: I think we should start with I.C. Here is the address of the destination. There's a good probability it would be the initial location. (*to Sam and Ella*) Do you mind if we make a copy of this ledger? It would aid us greatly.

SAM: Sure! Go ahead.

GOODMAN: (*looking in trunk*) We also need to get the coroner in on this and check out this body. See if he can approximate the time of death and the cause. I don't see anything on the surface that appears to be trauma marks. No visible wounds. No apparent gunshot or stab indications.

BADHAM: Could've been strangled. You know like in that one movie where they strangle the guy with a rope or something and then stuff him in a trunk.

GOODMAN: Hitchcock. Rope.

BADHAM: No, it was a "plain" rope, like ya get at the hardware store.

GOODMAN: Uh-huh.

BADHAM: So, where is the location of the last person to have the truck?

GOODMAN: Located at 141 East Baltimore. It's a place called..

IGGY: *(on phone -enters other side*) Genovese's South Side Tavern, can I help you?

(*Trixie -cocktail waitress w/ drink tray & glasses comes out -works room*)

BADHAM: Let's go check it out.

(*SAM and ELLA exit as GOODMAN and BADHAM cross down -Trunk can be removed during the following dialogue*)

NARRATOR: Inspector Badham and Detective Goodman preceded to 141 East Baltimore, the location of the last delivery, rental truck # 9 had made. Their intent was to question the owner of the initials IC and see what they knew about the trunk. In the meantime, the body was sent to the coroner's office and the trunk sent to the crime lab.

BADHAM : You know what I don't understand?

GOODMAN: Calculus?

BADHAM: In addition to that. I don't understand why somebody would be so careless? I mean, stuff a body in a trunk, put it on a rental trunk and then just leave it? What kinda silly brained forgetful wiseguy be so... forgetful?

GOODMAN: Well, that remains to be seen. Perhaps they left it in there for a reason.

BADHAM : I mean, if you're gunna kill somebody and dump the body and then leave them on a truck for somebody to find! I mean, what are the odds?

IGGY: (*on phone*) Twenty to one on "Irish Rose" in the fifth. Your best long shot is "Carbon Copy" at 50 to 1 in the sixth. Place to show, but it's showing rain, go with a strong mudder. Arlington's got clear skies.

Goodman and Badham enter bar area.

TRIXIE: Can I help yous guys?

GOODMAN: We're looking for a person with the initials.. I.C.

TRIXIE: I.C. ?

BADHAM: That's what the man said sister.

TRIXIE: Hey Iggy!

IGGY: Hang on a sec there Sal, (*puts phone down*) What is it Trixie?

TRIXIE: Ixnay on ookie-bay! Got a couple of op-kays here! They're lookin' for a mug with the initials I.C.

IGGY: Oh yea? What do they want?

TRIXIE: What do ya want?

BADHAM: A little compassion and understanding. World peace would be nice. But for right now we'd like to alk-tay to this I.C. ellow-fay.

TRIXIE: They want to talk to you Iggy.

IGGY: What for?

BADHAM: We want to know the answer to a big riddle, smart guy.

IGGY: A riddle? What is this? Some kinda joke?

BADHAM : No, wise guy funny man! The only joke around here is your prices on potato chips!

IGGY: Who are you guys?

BADHAM: We're the taxpayer's best friend pal, we're the law.

GOODMAN: I'm detective Goodman and this Inspector Badham. We're here to talk to someone with the initials I.C.

IGGY: What did I... what did he do?

BADHAM: He rented a truck from the "You-Do-It" office in Chicago and delivered something to this location. Problem was, he left "something" on the truck.

IGGY: *(into phone)* Sal, I gotta go. There's some people here. Yea, later. *(hangs up)*

GOODMAN: May we ask your name sir?

IGGY: My name? My name's Ignatius Clam. But everybody calls me Iggy.

GOODMAN: I see.

BADHAM: So, Mr. Iggy Clam, did you rent a moving truck recently? Such as the one I just alluded to, previously, earlier, before?

IGGY: Could be. I might have. What's it to ya?

BADHAM : What's it to us? What it to us? Listen here Mr. Iggy smart guy man! We could run you down on so many trumped charges your head'll spin! Now you better come clean on couple things! Be like a good little birdie and start singin!

GOODMAN: Detective! Please.

BADHAM. Sorry.

IGGY: Gotta lotta spunk for a broad with a badge.

GOODMAN: Yes, she's very spunk-ful. Were you in possession of a large steamer trunk?

IGGY: Steamer trunk? Ummmmmm.... No.

GOODMAN: May we ask what exactly your cargo was from (nearby city) to here?

IGGY: My cargo? My cargo was vending machines.

BADHAM: Vending machines.

IGGY: Yea pal, vending and amusement type. I attended a Amusement & Vending convention in (nearby city), I rode with a buddy of mine. I bought some stuff, rented the trunk and brought it back.

BADHAM: What exactly did you buy?

TRIXIE: We gotta Gomer Pyle Pinball machine, but one of the flippers sticks and the tilt is set too high. And we got a Donkey Kong! I just love that little Mario guy, don't you?

BADHAM: He's my hero.

GOODMAN: So there was no steamer trunk then?

IGGY: No siree pal, never saw no trunk.

BADHAM: You want to ponder that question a little longer there smart guy? Or else the only "horses" you'll be bettin on is "Queen's knight to Rook four" carved outta soap from State Pen!

IGGY: Oh wait! (*thinking*) Trunk...trunk.. you mean that big thing in the back?

BADHAM: Exactly. The big thing in the back Einstein! The big thing that looked like a big trunk.

IGGY: Well, yea, that big thing was in there when I got the truck. I thought it was suppose to be there, ya know, for like people "moving" stuff. A place to put "stuff".

BADHAM : What kind of "stuff"?

IGGY: Stuff. Clothes and all like that.

GOODMAN: So, you're saying it was already there.

IGGY: Yea. I'm saying it was already there.

BADHAM : The trunk?

IGGY: Yea, the trunk.

GOODMAN: In the truck?

IGGY: In the truck.

GOODMAN: I see.

BADHAM : Did you look in it?

IGGY: How could I? It was locked.

GOODMAN: So, you did try?

IGGY: Sure. But like I said, it was a no-can-doer. Sealed tight. Is there something wrong with the trunk officers?

BADHAM : There could be. And there could be something wrong with your story smart guy bookie fella.

GOODMAN: So you rented the truck in (nearby city)?

IGGY: Yep. The trunk was there was there when I got it.

GOODMAN: O.K. Well, I guess we have no further questions Mr. Clam. We'll be in touch.

IGGY: Wonderful. I'll look forward to it.

(*Badham and Goodman cross away*)

BADHAM: Oh great! That's just wonderful. You realize this is Federal matter now? We're gunna lose this case to them. Just because it crosses state lines. Isn't that just typical!

GOODMAN: I'll call the Bureau and have them do the check in (*nearby state*).

BADHAM: Finally, an interesting case. Why does the Bureau get to do all the cool stuff?!!

GOODMAN: Well, sometimes "interesting" can also be defined as "strange". I have an interesting feeling this one is going to be very strange.

(*GEORGE and MARTHA enter stage area*)

BADHAM: What makes you say that?

GOODMAN: Just a feeling. Come on, Badham I'll buy you a double latte.

BADHAM: Nah, I just want some coffee.

(exit out back as Muledeer and Sullen come on stage area)

NARRATOR: The bureau was notified of this odd case and two agents were assigned. Agents known for their forte in odd cases. They paid a visit to office of the You Do it Rental company.

SULLEN: Excuse me?

GEORGE: Yes, can I help you?

SULLEN: Is this the office of the "You Do It" trunk rental company?

MARTHA: Yes it is.

MULEDEER: *(flipping badges)* I'm Agent Muledeer and this is Agent Sullen, we're with the bureau. You must be Mr. and Mrs. Albee.

GEORGE: Call me George.

MARTHA: Call me Martha.

GEORGE: I do hope there's no trouble.

MULEDEER: We were notified by the *(your town)* PD, that a truck rented from your location contained a steamer trunk.

MARTHA: A steamer trunk?

SULLEN: Yes and in this trunk were the remains of an unidentified middle aged man.

MULEDEER: The truck was rented from you two weeks ago by a Mr. Ignatius Clam, truck number 9.

SULLEN: Mr. Clam claims the trunk was there, when he rented from you.

GEORGE: A body?

MARTHA: A trunk!

GEORGE: Oh my word!

MARTHA: Oh my lands!

GEORGE: Holy cow!

MARTHA: Oh my goodness.

SULLEN: We'd like to know if either of you recall anything about this particular truck. And a trunk being left on it? Maybe by the previous renter?

MULEDEER: Or perhaps one of you may recall flashing lights from the sky late one night. Multi colored lights and maybe a bright white beam...

SULLEN: Agent Muledeer.

MULEDEER: Kind of like a tractor beam coming from a silvery cigar shaped object in the sky. Maybe it lowered a container onto one of your trucks.

SULLEN: Agent Muledeer.

MULEDEER: What?!

MARTHA: No! I didn't see any tractor beam.

GEORGE: I did see a tractor pull one time. Down at the civic center.

SULLEN: That's fine Mr. Albee, but we need to know if you remember anything about Truck number 9.

GEORGE: (*thinking*) Truck number 9.. number 9 .. number 9...

SULLEN: Here's a photo of the previous renter. (*hands to them*) Mr. Clam.

GEORGE: Oh yea! Truck number 9! I do recall something about this. I am recalling that a peculiar woman and a strange man brought it back late. Remember Martha? And this Mr. Clam fellow was in a bit of a rush. He had amusement machines or something that he had to pick up.

MARTHA: Oh yes, of course! And you had just rented out the last truck to little blonde, without doing a proper credit check. Just because she smiled at you.

GEORGE: I did not.

MARTHA: Did too!.

GEORGE: Did not! Did not! It was a smirk, not a smile.

MARTHA: Whatever Georgie! Anyway, we couldn't help this Clam character. And he made quite a scene about it. And just then, that woman and the strange man came roaring back, in number 9 !

GEORGE: And that Clam fellow grabbed it up, *as is* and took off! Without you doing a proper credit check either, as I recall.

MARTHA: Oh stop it George.

SULLEN: So anyway, he took it "As is", huh? No one checked the truck out?

GEORGE: No. The Clam fellow wanted it there and then. He just put down the cash signed the papers and off he went. I believe there was a smile involved also.

MARTHA: I'm warning you George!

GEORGE: Warn away Martha. Warn away. See if care.

MULEDEER: So, no one looked in the truck to see if it was completely empty, correct?

MARTHA: That's correct, young man. Usually we have our son check out the trucks. But this time he didn't have a chance. You really should meet our son, he's such a wonderful boy.

GEORGE; Martha!

MARTHA: Sorry, George.

MULEDEER: So anything could have been in that truck? Such as a large steamer trunk?

GEORGE: Yes indeed.

MULEDEER: Or a cargo of alien bodies, in small steel containers, that had crash landed in the desert near Utah. Hidden there by the government?

GEORGE: Anything is possible.

SULLEN: (*clears throat*) So, about this "lady" who brought the truck back, (*checking her notes*) was... Madame Dane Du Boyse?

GEORGE: (*checking his ledger*) Let's see.. yep, here it is..Du Boyse. Strange woman.

MARTHA: Two weeks late she was! Was suppose to turn the truck in on the 4th, didn't get it back until the 18th.

GEORGE: Yea. Had some sordid story about....

MULEDEER: About alien abduction and a Government cover up?

GEORGE: No, that a she had lost the truck and that's why she was late.

SULLEN: Lost the truck?

GEORGE: Something like that. Anyway, she finally found it and brought it back.

MARTHA: Two weeks late she was.

SULLEN: What do think Agent?

MULEDEER: I think we need to check this lady out.

SULLEN: Right. We should also notify Detective Goodman and Badham that the trunk may go back farther than (*nearby city*).

(*GOODMAN and BADHAM enter Badham has cell phone*)

MULETEER: Thank you Mr. Albee.

GEORGE: Thank you.

GEORGE and MARTHA exit - MULEDEER and SULLEN cross far SL /Sullen dials out on cell phone.

BADHAM: (*into phone*) So, (*nearby city*) was a dead end huh?

SULLEN: Well, it may have been the "dead" beginning, but no one here checked the truck. Apparently it was rented too fast. But we have a lead on the previous renter. Agent Muledeer and I are going to check it out.

BADHAM: Well good. I hope it ends there, because you know this thing could turn out to be a real Energizer Bunny here, it keeps going and going and going... We could end up tracing this thing all the way to Timbuktu.

SULLEN: According to the records, this lady rented the truck in New Orleans..

BADHAM: New Orleans!?

SULLEN: Yes, and evidently it was lost for awhile.

BADHAM: Lost? How can someone lose a truck?

SULLEN: We'll we're going to try to find out. Did you find out anything new on the body?

BADHAM: Yea. Goodman's got the goods on that. Hang on. (*hands phone to Goodman*) Here, it's that FBI broad, she wants to know the status on the stiff.

GOODMAN: Hello, Agent Sullen?

SULLEN: So what the story on our victim?

GOODMAN: Well, apparently everything. The coroner found poison in his system. Arsenic and cyanide. Also he found knife wounds and gunshots in his back. Whoever wanted our person dead, certainly took extreme measures.

MULEDEER: Ask him if they found evidence of a probe.

SULLEN: Anything on the time of death?

GOODMAN: He narrowed it down to be about two to three weeks.

MULEDEER: Ask him about the probe!

SULLEN: (*tries to cover phone*) Shut up!

GOODMAN: I'm sorry?

SULLEN: Nothing. It's was just... a thing.. uh.. any identity on body yet?

GOODMAN: Not yet. They're still checking dental records. As soon as we get a positive ID we will know more. Maybe someone can identify him from a photo. Perhaps a relative or a friend. We can bring them into the morgue for the remains to be seen. We'll keep you posted.

SULLEN: Thank you detective. We'll be in touch. (*disconnects*)

MULEDEER: So, what's the story?

SULLEN: Well, it's a homicide all right. The victim was poisoned, stabbed and shot.

MULEDEER: But not probed huh? No little transmitters hidden on the back of the neck?

SULLEN: No, agent. This is a normal investigation. There is no "para" in this one.

MULEDEER: Right Sullen. A middle aged man is poisoned, shot and stabbed, stuffed in a trunk and has been floating around the country in a rental truck for weeks now, and no one knows anything about it. It just seemed to "be there" the whole time. That's normal?

SULLEN: Well, ... It can be.

MULEDEER: Right!

SULLEN: O.K. When we go see this lady, let me do the talking. If you say anything, it better not be anything about aliens, or cover ups or anything goofy, all right?

MULEDEER: All right, all right. Let's go.

(*They exit off left*)

MADAME DuBOYS enters from right holding martini glass and cigarette holder.

MADAME: Noel? Noel? Where are you, you dreadful thing! I must get my affairs in order! There are a lot of loose ends to be tied up this evening! What good is having a personal assistant when they are never around to assist you?! Noel? Noel!

NOEL: *(enters also holding martini glass)* Yes, madam?

MADAME: Now, I wanted you in here for something.... and now I don't recall.

NOEL: Another drink madam?

MADAME: Of course, that must have been it.

NOEL: *(turns to leave -stops -turns back)* Oh yes, I almost forgot. There are some people here to see you about.... something.

MADAME: People? Here? Something?

NOEL: Something like that. I think they said something about...something. Questions, I believe was mentioned at some point.

MADAME: Questions? Are they from the press? Who are they with? ABC? NBC? CBS?

NOEL: Ummmm... FBI.

MADAME: FBI? What is that? Fox Broadcasting Incorporated?

MULDEDEER and SULLEN enter.

MULEDEER: Federal Bureau of Investigation

NOEL: Yep. That's it! *(exits)*

MADAME: Investigation? What is this about? Who are you?

SULLEN: I'm agent Sullen and this agent Muledeer. We're here to ask you some questions about a truck you rented from the "You Move It" Truck Rental company.

MADAME: A truck?

MULEDEER: Yes, a truck. A truck that you apparently moved cargo from New Orleans to here.

MADAME: Yes, yes, I recall. I lived in New Orleans for a while. I stayed with my sister Stella and her awful husband Stanley. But I had no desire to remain there.

SULLEN: So you did indeed rent a truck. Trunk number 9?

MADAME: Yes, I needed a truck. I have a lot possessions you know. Many costumes and such. I am a member of the theatrical community. I have played all the great roles. Surely, you must of heard of me, Madame Dane Du Boyse!

SULLEN: No, I'm sorry. We don't get out much.

MADAME: Out! Out! Damn spot!

MULEDEER: That's very good. Macbeth right?

MADAME: (*indicating offstage*) No, my dog Spot. Get out! Out!

SULLEN: Now about this truck...

MADAME: I admit, I have been away from the stage and screen for a while, but I am about to make my glorious comeback! My agent has been talking to Steven Spielburg and plans are in the works for a feature film, with yours truly! My assistant has the details, Noel?! Noel! I swear, Noel is such a coward.

SULLEN: About the truck Miss Du Boyse.

MADAME: Truck?

SULLEN: The truck you rented to move here.

MADAME: Yes, yes. The dreadful truck. After all a woman of my stature driving a horrid truck! But who knows when you can use the experience, perhaps a role may demand it

MULEDEER: Do you recall anything unusual in the truck?

MADAME: Well, there was an unusual smell! But I believe it was Noel. He has a hygiene problem.

SULLEN: May I ask, were you in possession of a large steamer trunk?

MADAME: I am in possession of many trunks! I have kept all my costumes from over the years! I have the dress I wore in "Shoreman Takes A Wife" and the outfit I wore in "Merchant Marine Follies". And of course there was the costume I wore in...

SULLEN: That's all well and good ma'am, but do you recall leaving a trunk on the truck? Is there one you may be missing?

MADAME: Missing? No. I have everything. All my trunks are accounted for. I took seven trunks and still have seven trunks. I think.

MULEDEER: You think? What do you mean?

MADAME: I am thinking there may have been eight at some point, for some reason. I know I only had seven. There may have been an extra.

SULLEN: An extra?

MADAME: Of course, I was an extra when I first started out. I was in the street scene "Holiday a Go Go", I was in the blue dress. That's actually how I was discovered. The head of MGM saw me in the background and asked...

SULLEN: About the *extra* trunk Miss Du Boyse. You said, you thought there may have been an extra trunk?

MADAME: Yes, yes of course. I think there were too many at one point, but that's when my friends borrowed it at some small town somewhere, I think.

MULEDEER: Your friends borrowed the truck? The office in (*nearby city*) said you had "lost" it.

MADAME: No, no. I only told them I lost it. Just pretending. Acting you know. I thought it may look bad if I told them, I lent it out to some friends. Although, making something up on the spur of the moment is not my strong point. I am not one for improvisation. I need lines, I need direction.

MULEDEER: All right, here's your scene. You're in a rental trunk. You've been driving all night, your hands wet on the wheel.

MADAME: Yes? And the voice in my head that drives my heel?

MULEDEER: Could be. Now, you're somewhere. A small town somewhere. Maybe you've just pulled over to rest... and... action!

MADAME: Yes, well, Noel and I pulled over for.... some libations. I was never one for the road you know. Although. I did travel extensively with the touring company of My Little Pony On Ice, and we had these awful buses with absolutely no...

MULEDEER: And so there you are at a some small town... you're wanting libations...

MADAME: Oh yes... and anyway, there we were in this ghastly hotel bar.. .er ...libation establishment, when low and behold I ran into a dear old stage friend of mine, who was currently touring the country with a musical review. Well, it seems her station wagon had broken down and she was in dire straits.

SULLEN: So, you lent them your truck?

MADAME: Only for a week. She agreed to bring it straight back to me when they were finished. So, Noel and I hopped the next train and came here.

MULEDEER: Did you take your cargo with you?

MADAME: Only what I could manage. The rest she and her friend agreed to bring with them. They said it wouldn't be in the way.

SULLEN: Did you leave your trunks on the truck?

MADAME: No, I only left four. . Noel and I managed to bring the other four ahead.

MULEDEER: But I thought you only had seven.

MADAME: Well, that the amusing thing. That is the extra one that I spoke of. I know we had only packed seven in New Orleans, but at some point there were eight, I forget why.

SULLEN: You're positive you only had seven.

MADAME: Yes. I am certain of it. I believe I am certain of it. I cannot explain the extra one. If indeed there was an extra one. Maybe there wasn't. Or maybe Noel had it. He has a lot of baggage.

NOEL: (*entering*) No, mam. I only had a carry on to.. carry on. I am not in the way of having ... the need of a trunk.

SULLEN: So, your friends brought the truck here to you.

MADAME: Yes, I believe they were a teensy bit late.

MULEDEER: And who unpacked the truck it when it arrived?

MADAME: Noel did.

SULLEN: And there were *four* trunks on the truck?

NOEL: Yes, but I only unload three. The three that belonged to.... what's her face there.

SULLEN: How did you know which "three" belonged to Madame DuBoys?

NOEL: Because, all of her trunks are a horrid lavender color and reek of mothballs. That's all I'm loaded.. I unloaded.. from the.. off the... truck.

MULEDEER: Do you recall an extra one?

NOEL: Maybe but.. I'm a personal assistant, not a extra trunk figure outer.. fixing person.. .guy.

MULEDEER: So you may have left an extra trunk on the truck?

NOEL: You're darn tootin' sparky.

MULEDEER: And if there was a extra trunk, neither of you would have any idea where it came from?

NOEL: Maybe Captain Kirk beamed it down.

MULEDEER: Really?

NOEL: As if!

SULLEN: So, let me see if we got this straight. In New Orleans, you loaded seven trunks. Somewhere between there and someplace near here, you picked up and extra one?

NOEL: No, it was between here and there.

SULLEN: That's what I said.

NOEL: That's correct.

MULEDEER: Do you think these friends of yours may have loaded this extra trunk?

MADAME: I don't know.

MULEDEER: Do you recall the name of this small town where you stopped for the libations?

MADAME: The small town? No. I have no earthly idea. Though, I believe there's a school there.

MULEDEER: A school?

MADAME: Yes, (*major university nearby*)

MULEDEER: Oh. Yea. that's certainly is a school.

SULLEN: These friends that you lent the truck to, do you know where they are now?

MADAME: Heavens no. They were on tour. Could be anywhere.

MULEDEER: They didn't mention anything about the next city they were going to?

MADAME: It may have been Milwaukee. Or Sheboygan. I don't recall.

SULLEN: Think Miss DuBoys. Think!

NOEL: Sheboygan.

SULLEN: Sheboygan? That's where they were headed?

NOEL: I don't know, I just like saying that. Sheboygan! It's fun.

MADAME: But what is this all about? Why these questions? What is it, with this trunk?

MULEDEER: It's a highly top secret federal matter ma'am. We're not at liberty to discuss the details at this time.

NOEL: Sheboygan!

MADAME: Well, I demand to know more that you're telling me! Before I say another thing or answer any more questions, I should like to know what this investigation is about.

SULLEN: As agent Muledeer said, it's a closed matter at this moment.

MADAME: Well, that would never play in Peoria. (*gasps*) That's it! They were going to Peoria!

NOEL: Sheboygan!

SULLEN: Poughkeepsie?

NOEL: Sheboygan!

SULLEN: Thank you very much mam, we may have more questions later.

They exit quickly off left

MULEDEER: We'll be in touch.

MADAME: I refuse to tell you anything more until you tell me.... where did they go?

NOEL: Peoria?

MADAME: What on earth was that all about anyway?

NOEL: Don't know. Another drink mam?

MADAME: Of course!

they begin exiting right.

MADAME: How was my performance Noel?

NOEL: Sheboygan.

MADAME: (*stops turns*) I'm ready for my closeup Mr. Spielberg! (*exits*)

NARRATOR: Agents Muledeer and Sullen hopped onto the long and winding road, which only seemed to become... longer and windier. Would they find what they needed in Poughkeepsie? Well, it remains to be seen. In the meantime, Detective Goodman and Inspector Badham found startling new evidence about the body from the trunk. (*exits*)

GOODMAN & BADHAM enter stage

BADHAM: Well, I just talked to the FBI broad again, they think they may have a lead on where the trunk came from. They're on their way to Peoria now.

GOODMAN: Peoria huh? The trail widens.

BADHAM; It's like I said, this thing could lead all the way back to who's knows where. That trunk may have been floatin in the back of that trunk for years!

GOODMAN: But at least we have a positive ID on the victim now. He was an investigative reporter for the Hungry Eye Herald. From what we know, he was doing research on for illegal gaming in the (*tri state*) area. The use of illegal Poker machines and video Slot machines in various establishments.

BADHAM: I'm tellin' ya, it sounds like a Mob hit to me! Ten to one will get ya our buddy Iggy and the stooges, down at Genovese's tavern.

GOODMAN: But then again, one of his associates said, he was also working on a piece about highway safety. He was profiling various trucking companies. One of his angels was the rental industry. The "do it yourself" line.

BADHAM: You mean like the "You Do it" Rentals Trucks?

GOODMAN: Ten four. Apparently, a lot of these mom and pop operations don't keep their fleet up to code.

BADHAM: So, he was working on story about both? Illegal Vending machines and shoddy truck rentals? So, at this point it could be anybody!

GOODMAN: That's a very large affirmative.

BADHAM: So, not only is this trunk leading us everywhere, but so is the M.O. This is just beautiful. Just swell!

GOODMAN: Well, maybe Peoria well shed some light on it.

BADHAM: I certainly hope so. If not, I'm gunna need a scorecard to keep track of all the players.

GOODMAN: Come on Inspector, I'll buy you coupla glazed crawlers and cup of joe.

BADHAM: Swell. A human can never have enough sugar and caffeine! *(they exit)*

ANNOUNCER VOICE: Ladies and Gentleman, welcome to the Fabulous Kabookie Room of the Holiday Inn, in lovely downtown Peoria. For your dining and dancing pleasure this evening, we present the song stylings of Edie Buffet and friends!! Please put your hands together, for Ms. Edie Buffet!

(Edie enters -holding microphone)

EDIE: Thank you! Thank you! You're too kind. Thank you. As you know, I'm Edie Buffet and welcome to this Holiday Inn here off route 29. I'll let you in on a little secret, as you may or may not know, I've been traveling somewhat solo the past several months. My wonderful and talented husband, the fabulous Shecky Scagnetti has been on.. somewhat of a hiatus. But I did speak to his lawyer this morning, and I'm please to announce, my dear Shecky may be back with us in a year to six months. Isn't that wonderful! And just as a helpful reminder, be sure to get your taxes in on time next month O.K.? O.K. enough said. At this point, I'd like to bring out the person who has helped me cope for the past several weeks, I discovered him at Karaoke bar and I think he is just sensational. What a talent. What a voice. What a smile. Please, welcome, the very talented Nick Niagara!

NICK: *(enters - beings singing "It not unusual" -couple of bars- throwing in "Hey" etc. to audience.*

EDIE: Isn't he just the cat's meow ladies?

NICK: (*sings*) What's new pussycat, whoa-oh-oh -whoa-oh!

EDIE: (*to lady in audience*) What do you think ma'am? Should I keep him? (play *off whatever she says -if anything*) So, what's your name? Where are you from? Anyone else here from.....? (*play off that - a maybe a few others - then approach SULLEN*) Hello mam, what's your name , where are you from?

SULLEN: I'm Agent Sullen. I'm from the FBI.

EDIE: Oh! The FBI? Anyone else here from the FBI?

MULEDEER: I am.

EDIE: So! Both of you are from the FBI, isn't that wonderful?

NICK: (*sings*) Secret - Agent man! Secret - agent man.

SULLEN: I have a few questions for you Mrs. Buffet.

EDIE: Isn't that sweet, the little FBI girl has some questions.

SULLEN: Did you borrow a truck from a Madame Dane DuBoys recently?

EDIE: DuBoys? Well, yes I sure did.

MULEDEER: And this would be near (*nearby city*) ?

NICK. (*sings*) School's out for summer. School's out forever! Hey!

SULLEN: And then drove it back to her in (nearby city)?

NICK: (*sings*) On the road again , just can't wait....

EDIE: As a matter of fact, yes we did. Madame DuBoys was such a sweetheart.

MULEDEER: Did you have any luggage Mrs. Buffet..

EDIE: Please, darling call me Edie.

MULEDEER; Did you have any luggage? Such as a large steamer trunk?

EDIE: Honey, I've had a million steamer trunks and lord only knows where they are now. I'm losing them all the time. You arrive in St. Paul, your luggage arrives in Dallas. You go to Dallas, your luggage goes to Miami.

SULLEN: Did you have any luggage when you borrowed Madame Duboys truck?

EDIE: Possibly. I'm not sure. I believe we had a few things. But really hon, we're trying to do a show here for these lovely people. Maybe you should come and see me during the break.

MULEDEER: When is the break?

EDIE: Well, our show lasts for two hours and twenty minutes.

NICK: (*sings*) Ti-igh ime. Is on our side. Yes it is.

MULEDEER: You mean, we'd have to sit and listen to this guy for two more hours?

NICK: Hey pal, what'dya mean by that?

MULEDEER: I mean, that I've seen more entertaining alien autopsies. I've heard more soulful tunes coming out of demonically possessed postal workers.

EDIE: That's no way to talk to little Nickie.

MULEDEER: I believe we need a break *now*, don't you agent Sullen?

SULLEN: Indeed I do, agent Muledeer.

MULEDEER: O.K. Break time! Everybody take five. Have some pudding or something.

EDIE: But.. wait! I wanted to try my new Celine Dion retrospective!

SULLEN: Come with us Mrs. Buffet. We have a few more questions for you. (*leading away*)

MULEDEER: Come on Mr. Nick, you too. (*leads him away*)

NICK: (*sings*) And now the end is near.. and so I face the final curtain...

NARRATOR: (*insert whatever announcement you need i.e. dessert or intermission etc.*)

END OF ACT ONE

ACT TWO

BADHAM, GOODMAN, SULLEN and MULEDEER come on stage - Badham pacing w/ coffee. They stage talk under the following narrative.

NARRATOR: Welcome back. When we last left our heroes, they were pursuing the evil badman into Dry man's gulch... sorry, wrong story. Oh yes! I remember! The case of the wandering trunk had covered many miles in this strange case, without turning up a solid lead or clue. This mystery had the authorities baffled, not to mention, certain people in the audience . The interrogation of Edie Buffet and Nick Niagra had turned up nothing. Neither of them recalled a steamer trunk being on the truck at the time. Edie did recall a peculiar odor being on the truck, but believed it had something to do Nick's socks. In the meantime, Detective Goodman and Inspector Badham spent many a long night over donuts and coffee, pondering this perplexing case of impervious platitude.

BADHAM: So, no one knows "zip" about our trunk? Is that it?

SULLEN: Well, apparently not. At least nothing we can confirm. Someone, somewhere isn't telling us the truth.

MULEDEER: But as we all know... the truth is out there.

BADHAM: All right, let's go over it all again. A, we have a dead investigative journalist, a Mr. Howard Pepper, who was murdered and then put in a trunk and left on the back of a rental truck.

GOODMAN: Yes. And the trunk containing his body was discovered at the return location of the U Do it truck rental in (your town). The workers who discovered the body, both check out. Despite a few outstanding parking tickets, they're harmless. The trunk arrived after being driven here by an Ignatious Clam.

BADHAM: Who may or may not have been transporting illegal vending machines from (nearby city). And according to him, the trunk was all ready on the truck when he got it. Then we jump back to (nearby city), where the rental people up there don't know nothing except the truck was supposedly "lost".

MULEDEER: And the supposedly "lost" rental truck wasn't "lost". It was "lent". Lent out to some lounge lizards who claim they only had a few suitcases, two turntables and a microphone.

SULLEN: Edie Buffet and Nick Niagara claim they never used the cargo section of the truck, nor did they look in there. For all they know, the trunk was in there, when they borrowed it from Madame DuBoys.

MULEDEER: And DuBoys and her assistant Noel claim they had seven trunks when the left New Orleans, which checks out with our agents in New Orleans. The Rental Office said the truck was clean when it left there.

BADHAM: They're sure?

MULEDEER: Positive. When I say, "clean" we're talking literally. Truck Number 9 was "washed" and "cleaned" before DuBoyse rented it. There was no "trunk" there. It only appears somewhere in between there and here.

BADHAM: So, it has to be DuBoys! Either that or somebody slipped them extra trunk when they weren't looking.

MULEDEER: Can I just point out at this point, that we shouldn't dismiss extraterrestrial involvement in this case.

SULLEN: Agent. Don't start.

MULEDEER: Come on Sullen, look at the facts. No one knows anything about this trunk. It's as if, it just "appeared"! Well, maybe that's because it did. Maybe this reporter, this Howard Pepper guy was out on some lost highway and...and.. .

SULLEN: And he stumbled upon a UFO landing sight, He moved in to get a better look and was discovered by these aliens. They grabbed him, erased his memory, and for good measure fed him poison, stabbed him, shot him, stuffed him in a trunk and dropped him on a passing rental truck.

MULEDEER: It could happen.

BADHAM: Oh yea. And monkey's will fly outta my nose.

GOODMAN: I believe we need to look at the actual facts more closely. I am under the assumption that there are clues somewhere within the trail.

BADHAM: Clues? Where? I don't see any clues! Knock knock, who's there? No clues!

GOODMAN: Well, let's look at the murder victim, the late Mr. Howard Pepper. We know the investigative stories he had been working on, were confined to this region. This is confirmed from the notes we found on his person, and by the editor of the paper. We have no confirmation that he traveled to (nearby city), New Orleans or (city). That of course, narrows it down. Whatever happened, must have happened here or around here.

SULLEN: So, maybe the murderer committed the crime here, and then put him in this trunk, loaded him on the truck, with the hopes that he would end up far away. Like in some distant city, such as.. ..

MULEDEER: Sheboygan.

(gets a look from Sullen)

MULEDEER: Sorry. But it *is* fun to say.

BADHAM: So what you're saying is, someone intended for the body to end up as far away from here as possible. In hopes it would never be traced to the original location?

SULLEN: Right. As far away from the actual murder scene as possible.

BADHAM: So, it was just a stroke of bad luck that ended coming back here?

GOODMAN: But we cannot ignore the possibility that maybe the killer or killers, are not from this area.

MULEDEER: Precisely! I'm betting they're from the Klacktoo galaxy, in the M-5 nebula.

SULLEN: Agent!

MULEDEER; O.K. I was just joking that time.

BADHAM: What about the crime lab, did they get anything on that trunk? Any fingerprints?

SULLEN: Apparently, there are no other fingerprints on it except for the workers who carried it into the U Do It office. However, there was one interesting find inside the trunk. Evidently, the victim or someone, attempted to scratch a message into the underside lid.

BADHAM: A message? What did it say?

MULEDEER: From what the handwriting experts can tell, there is an "A" and a "C".

BADHAM: A & C? A & C? You sure it wasn't an "I" and a "C"?

SULLEN: No, they believe it is an "A". (*to Muledeer*) And before you say anything agent, A C doesn't stand for Alien Contact.

MULEDEER: I wasn't even going there.

SULLEN: Good. And here's one more interesting item we uncovered, before our victim's foray into the investigative reporting field, he was a "theatrical" critic.

BADHAM: Oh wonderful. That just opens the list of suspects up to the size of a football field. O.K. that's it! I've had it up to here with this goofy case. Tomorrow, I'm going back to something easier like...vice squad.

GOODMAN: Actually, I think it may narrow down our list.

BADHAM: Does anybody want to know what I think? I think we need to issue warrants on the whole lot of them and extradite all their keisters here! Put all their shiny happy faces up under the lights and see what they really have to say.

GOODMAN: Well, actually, I've already seen to that.

BADHAM: What? You have?

GOODMAN: Yes. I've put through the necessary paperwork and had everyone connected with the trunk, extradited to our fair city. In fact, they all should be arriving down at the station anytime now.

BADHAM: You hauled 'em all in? Really! Well, what we standing around here for? Let's go!

GOODMAN: Very well.

   (they exit)

SULLEN: Any thoughts on this whole thing?

MULEDEER: Uh.. well...

SULLEN: *(cutting off)* That don't have anything do with little green men, government cover ups or supernatural phenomena.

MULEDEER: I have a few ideas. A few normal ideas.

SULLEN: Really?

MULEDEER: Yes really. I think our reporter stumbled onto something big. Whether it was the gambling story or highway thing, I think it was something bigger. I think "A .

C" is the answer. If we can figure out what that means, I think we'll have an answer.

SULLEN: But what does A.C. mean? Alternating Current? Ante Christum? Air Conditioning?

MULEDEER: It could be something obscure. Maybe it was all that he time to scratch. Maybe he wasn't finished. Maybe A C where only the first to letters.

SULLEN: Hmmm. Well, we can discuss it on the way to the station.

MULEDEER: All right. But I want to make a stop before we get down to the station. There are some old friends I want to see.

SULLEN: Who? It's not that UFO Conspiracy convention is it?

(*they begin exiting*)

MULEDEER: And by the way, the little men aren't green. They're more of a burnt umber.

(*they exit - NICK and EDIE enter*)

EDIE: This is outrageous! We are suppose to be playing the VFW in Hoboken this very evening! Instead we're in some awful police station. Now, I know what my poor Shecky must be going through. I know he feels now.

NICK: (*singing*) Feelings. Nothing more than feelings..

MADAME: *(enters)* What is that dreadful noise in here? Sounds like someone sitting on ferret! (*seeing Edie*) Oh! Edie!

EDIE: Dane DuBoys! What on earth!!

(*they run and hug - Hollywood kiss -kiss*)

MADAME: I never thought I'd see the day, when people such as ourselves would be herded into a place such as this, like common criminals! What is all this business about anyway?

EDIE: I think it has something to do with truck you lent us.

MADAME: Why? Because we returned it late? I have some overdue periodicals from the library as well! Will they throw the book at me? Oh! Woah is me! It's off to the big house with me!

NOEL: (*enters*) Madame?

MADAME: Oh Edie, you know my personal assistant and accountant, Noel.

EDIE: Yes of course!

NOEL: Madame, I checked, but the bar isn't open here.

MADAME: Of course not, you nincompoop! This is a police station. The only bars in here, are the ones you stand behind.

NOEL: I'd much rather stand in front of one ma'am, if you don't mind. Thank you very much.

MADAME: Yes, yes. Very well. Do whatever you want.

NOEL: Thank you. But first, I think I need a little nappy poo. (*lays down -curls up*)

MADAME: Noel, Noel! Get up off the floor.

NICK: (*sings*) Sweet dreams till sunbeams find you. Sweet dreams that leave your worries behind you.

EDIE: Nick! You can cut the crap.

NICK: Crap? But I love singing.

EDIE: Yea. I've noticed. And it's starting to get on my last nerve.

NICK: You mean, you don't like my voice?

EDIE: Your voice is fine, it's your singing that's giving me hives.

IGGY: (*offstage sings few bars of Luck Be A Lady*)

EDIE: I take that back Nick, you're improving.

NICK: But that wasn't me.

EDIE: Well, who was it?

IGGY: (*enters*)Well, well, well. Look at this lot. I thought this was a police line up, not a Fellini castin call.

EDIE: Was that *you* singing?

IGGY: Yea. Sorry. I'm so happy I could just sing.

MADAME: I demand to know why they brought us here!

BADHAM and GOODMAN enter

BADHAM: All right people, simmer! Someone want to wake up sleeping beauty there?

MADAME: I demand to know why we have been brought here!

EDIE: Yea! Nick and I have gig that we're missing tonight.

IGGY: Yea, what gives doll? You can't hold us here unless you charge us with something.

BADHAM: Get this straight Mr. Clam guy mouth man, first off I ain't your doll. And second ot all, you're all under suspicion.

EDIE: Suspicion? Suspicion of what?

GOODMAN: Suspicion of the murder of Mr. Howard Pepper.

MADAME-EDIE-IGGY: Murder??!!

BADHAM: That's right. Until one of you coughs up a better story about the traveling trunk, we're holding you for as long as we feel like it.

IGGY: You can't do that! It ain't constitutional. Besides, I told you that trunk was on the truck when I got it.

GOODMAN: But why did it take you so long to remember that Mr. Clam? When inspector Badham and I questioned you, you didn't even recall a trunk being on the truck.

IGGY: I had a lot on my mind. I didn't know what you guys were talkin' about.

BADHAM: Didn't know what we were talkin' about huh?

MADAME; I still don't know what you're talking about. What trunk? What murder?

GOODMAN: The extra trunk that appeared on your rental truck, Miss DuBoys. Agent Muledeer and agent Sullen spoke with you about it in (*nearby city*).

MADAME: Oh that. I told them and I'm telling you, I only had seven trunks.

GOODMAN: But you said, you recalled eight at some point. Somewhere near (*nearby city*).

MADAME: Perhaps I was seeing double when I looked at one. All that driving makes one eyes do funny things.

BADHAM: So are you denying your original story? Are you saying there was only seven now?

MADAME: Seven little indians, all in a row..

GOODMAN: We have you on record mam, stating that you saw an extra trunk at some point. Around the time you lent the truck to Ms Buffet.

MADAME: Well then, proceed to ask her about it. Perhaps she put it there.

EDIE: I didn't put anything anywhere. I never even opened the back of the truck.

NICK: I thought you did.

EDIE: What?

BADHAM: What?

NICK: I thought you opened it when we was near (*nearby city*).

EDIE: I didn't open it in (*nearby city*).

NICK: Oh. I thought you did.

GOODMAN: Did you see someone open it Mr. Niagra?

NICK: I thought so.

EDIE: Well, it wasn't me!

NICK: Maybe I didn't.

EDIE: Oh I see! You're just sore at me for making that crack about your singing.

NICK: No I'm not.

EDIE: Yes you are.

NICK: No I'm not.

BADHAM: Children! Children! Please! Would someone please wake up Otis over there?

Goodman goes and wakes Noel.

EDIE: All right little Nickie, then answer me this! Did I have a trunk before we got to (*nearby city*)?

NICK: Well, no.

EDIE: Then what makes you think I suddenly had one once we got there?

NICK: So, I was wrong. I just thought I saw someone open up the back of the truck.

BADHAM: Where were you when you "thought" you saw this?

NICK: I was in my room after our gig. I was looking out the hotel window.

GOODMAN: What time was it?

NICK: I don't know. Around 1 am.

EDIE: Well that proves it wasn't me! At that time I was trying to get our show money from the club owner and that seedy bar tender!

IGGY: Hey. Watch the "seedy" talk there cookie.

GOODMAN: What else did you see Mr. Niagra? Did you see this person putting something on the truck?

BADHAM: Like a large trunk?

NICK: No. It might have been a dream.

BADHAM: Oh! It was all a dream now! Is that it, Mr smart guy singing man?

NICK: Could be.

BADHAM: All right! That's it! I had it with this thing! We'll never get to the bottom of this! I give up!

GOODMAN: What are you saying?

BADHAM: I'm saying it would take an army to get to the bottom of this case!

MADAME: Army? I played with the USO for many years. I was in Korea and that other foreign place. Jerry Colonga and I had a cute little number we used to do. How did it go? (*begins humming*)

BADHAM: We're getting the run around here Goodman! They're a bunch of lunatics! And only a bunch of lunatics could possibly get to the bottom of this!

   MULEDEER and SULLEN enter

MULEDEER: O.K. Show time people. Let's get this interrogation underway.

GOODMAN: (*looking out*) Agent Muledeer?

MULEDEER: Yep it's me. And I brought along some friends. (*indicating the audience*)

IGGY: Hey, what's with all those people out there?

MULEDEER: Well, I thought you might have some difficulty getting to the bottom of this case, so I called in some extra help.

GOODMAN: Who are those people?

MULEDEER: Just some friends of mine I picked up at Science Fiction and UFO Convention down the road.

You want people who can get down the nitty gritty? People who have the capacity for amazing detail and useless trivia. Who can recite every episode number and title of every Star Trek ever made? People who over analyze the most mundane situations and can find a conspiracy at every turn? Well, I got 'em.

SULLEN: It's a crazy idea I know. I tried to stop him but...

MULEDEER: I've filled them all in on the details of the case, all the twists and turns and it's piqued their curiosity beyond capacity. They're all teaming with questions. I say we turn them loose on the suspects and I bet in 15 minutes we'll have some solid answers!

BADHAM: Well, what the heck! Turn 'em loose.

MULEDEER: All right my fellow devotees of truth, justice and the science fiction way, before you are all the prime suspects in this case. If you want to ask anything or have any matters cleared up, now is you chance. Does anyone have any questions? *(..etc.)*

(At this point - the actors must fend for themselves and respond to questions. Experience has shown us, sometimes the questions are slow in coming at first but then tend to snowball. Usually it's best to field at least 5 or so questions then wrap it up by saying -"One more question")
(To wrap up the questions:- Narrator enters-)

NARRATOR: Well, there are the details of the case. As abstract as they may be. We've learned.. *(sum up anything from the questioning)*. Perhaps you or someone you know has information about this case. We need you to share it now. These agents and policeman desperately need your help. If you will now, turn your attention to the resolution forms (*at your table*). Please indicate on the form which of the suspects you believe is guilty. We will give you a few moments, then we will be around to collect them. (*add /adjust anything to fit your production - the suspects may exit at this point - Badham, Goodman, Muledeer and Sullen may assist in collecting the verdicts*)

at the conclusion of the complete collection-

NARRATOR: Well, we've looked at your resolution forms and suggestions, and we're just as confused as before. But nonetheless, during the running of this evening's broadcast, some new information came to light. Some information they may finally solve this baffling case.

GOODMAN: (*entering*) Inspector Badham! Agent Muledeer! Agent Sullen! I have some information that may finally solve this baffling case!

BADHAM: (*enters*) Oh yea?

SULLEN: (*enters*) Information?

MULEDEER: (*enter*) What is it?

GOODMAN: I'd like to gather the suspects out here one last time. I think it will prove beneficial.

BADHAM: O.K. I need all the funny guy smart people out here! Pronto.

(*they all enter ad-libbing various reactions*)

BADHAM: All right. The floor is yours Goodman.

GOODMAN: I've uncovered some more information about our murdered reporter Howard Pepper. Apparently, we were under the impression that he didn't keep very good notes. From what we could discern, he was investigating illegal vending machines and substandard rental vehicles.

BADHAM: But he *was*, right?

GOODMAN: Yes, he was. And from our viewpoint this fact seemed to shed suspicion on everyone involved. Our problem was trying to narrow the big picture instead of looking at it as a whole. So, I did a little checking on the initials AC.

SULLEN: Well? What does AC mean?

GOODMAN: I'll get to that in a moment but first I must ask Madame Dubois if she recalls a scathing review Mr. Pepper wrote many years ago that pretty much ruined your career?

MADAME: Scathing review? Pepper? Never heard of him.

GOODMAN: Or you Ms Buffet? A review of you and your husband's performance reduced you to playing seedy hotel lounges, which in turn prompted your husband to fudge the taxes a little and landed him in a minimum security prison?

EDIE: Review? Fudge? Uh, no. I don't recall anything about that.

GOODMAN: How about you Mr. Clam? You yourself were a former nightclub performer who was lambasted by a review from Mr. Pepper and sent you on a downward spiral until you landed to the ranks of a (your town) bartender?

IGGY: What was his name? Pepper?

GOODMAN: It could've been mere coincidence that this one particular journalist was directly connected to you though his newspaper articles, and had an impact on our your lives. But this is what lead me to the big connection that took coincidence one step beyond.

BADHAM: Big connection?

SULLEN: Coincidence?

MULEDEER: One step beyond?

GOODMAN: Yes, yes and yes. It wasn't until I learned that Mr. Pepper had attended an alumni reunion at (nearby city) that it all fell into place.

BADHAM: Oh, I see. A reunion huh? Hmm.. these reunions are usually pretty big deals. Catered affairs. I would imagine they had a "bar" there. And who might have been tending bar at this event?

GOODMAN: A Mr. Ignatius Clam.

SULLEN: And they probably had entertainment of some sort? Maybe someone who was in town that would work cheap. I wonder who they may have hired?

GOODMAN: A Ms Edie Buffet and Nick Niagra.

MULEDEER: And I recall someone saying they stopped for "libations" at some small town with a school. And happen to run into some old theatrical friend?

GOODMAN: Madame Dane DuBoys.

IGGY: No way! You're not pinnin' this one on me!

MULEDEER: Oh we probably can. All we'd have to do is make a few phone calls and confirm that you were *all* at the alumni reunion.

GOODMAN: I already did.

MULEDEER: See that? He already did.

BADHAM: I bet two to one, everyone had on those little name tags. And someone saw "Hi! My Name is Howard Pepper". And someone recognized him. And someone struck up a conversation and confirmed he was the guy. The critic that spoiled your act.

MULEDEER: It was probably pure chance that you were all together at the same place and the same time. A once in a lifetime shot. You couldn't let this one opportunity slip by.

NOEL: And so you got revenge!!

MADAME: Noel! Shut up!!

IGGY: It was them, I tell ya! They planned it!

EDIE: We did not! *You* gave him the poison!

IGGY: Well you stabbed him!

EDIE: Well she shot him! (*pointing to Madame*)

IGGY: But you were suppose to *ditch* the trunk, not leave it on the truck!

EDIE: DuBoys said she would do it.

MADAME: Me? My assistant was suppose to take care of it before I returned it.

NOEL: *(remembering)* Oh yea! The trunk! Where did I put that thing?

MADAME: Nowhere you little dimwitted boob! You left it on the truck.

NOEL: Was I suppose to?

MADAME-EDIE-IGGY: NO!

NOEL: OK. OK . I'll do it tomorrow. Jeez.

BADHAM: Wait a minute. So, you mean... they "all" did it?

GOODMAN: Yes. That's what I mean.

NOEL: Wait a minute! Did I do it too?

EDIE: No, you were passed out in the front seat.

NOEL: Really? You mean I missed it all?

MADAME: No! You flubbed it all. If you had gotten rid of that trunk none of this would've happened!

NICK: So, it *was* you I saw!!

EDIE: Wow. You figured that out huh? I guess there are brains in the head of yours after all.

MADAME: You shall be hearing from my solicitors in the morning! This is an outrage! I'm to appear on the Johnny Carson show tomorrow night. He'll never stand for it!

SULLEN: I'll escort them down to processing.

IGGY: (*exiting*) I'll escort myself pal!

EDIE: (*exiting*) Now I can be with my Shecky again! We can tour all the prisons!

SULLEN: Come on folks lets go.

MADAME: You have to admit, I really did give a spectacular performance, didn't I?

SULLEN: It was wonderful. You're Oscar is waiting out there.

MADAME: Oh really? (*as she goes*) I'd like to thank the academy on behalf of...*etc*

(*they leave except for Noel and Nick*)

BADHAM: Hang on here a second, Goodman! How does AC fit into all of this?

GOODMAN: Well, I got a search warrant for Mr. Pepper's apartment. I happened to notice just as I was leaving, there was book laying in a chair by a reading lamp.

BADHAM: Yea? So?

GOODMAN: It was, "Murder on the Orient Express" by Agatha Christie.

BADHAM: So?

GOODMAN: A.C. Agatha Christie.

BADHAM: Yea, so?

GOODMAN: So, in the conclusion of this particular book, *all* the suspects are guilty. They *all* did it.

BADHAM: So, you mean to tell me, Pepper scratched "AC" just before he died in hopes that someone would figure that out?

GOODMAN: As best as I can tell, yes.

BADHAM: It's a little obscure don't you think? Couldn't he just have scratched 'They All did It" ?

GOODMAN: There probably wasn't time. After all, he had been poisoned, stabbed and shot.

BADHAM: Oh yea. Good point. But what about the trunk?

GOODMAN: From what I can tell, that's the amusing thing. It was an unfortunate happenstance that Mr. Clam rented the truck that he did. Fate put him at the that rental office at the right time. For all he knew, that truck had been return two weeks earlier.

BADHAM: That's right! DuBoyse brought back two weeks late. Wow! I guess it's like they say Goodman, what goes around, comes around.

NICK: Speaking of coming around, are we free to go?

GOODMAN: Sure.

(*Goodman and Badham exit*)

NICK: (*to Noel*) So, you need a lift somewhere?

NOEL: Naw, I'm gunna wait.

NICK: You're gunna wait? Wait for what?

NOEL: Goddot.

NICK: Oh. (*Nick Exits*)

(*Narrator enters*)

NARRATOR: A small police station in *(Your town)*. Four investigators stumble upon a body inside a trunk. It leads them to and fro and back again. A trunk that took a journey from point A to point B and back to A again. Was it fate that brought Mr. Howard Pepper back again? Or was it a distance force that transcends both logic and.... that other thing. Did the trunk journey from (your town*)* to (nearby city) to (Cambridge) and back to (your town)? Or did this trunk, journey somewhere beyond. Down the long dark highways, of the mystery zone. (*beat*) Beats me. (*exits*)

NOEL: (*looks around for moment -pulls small electronic type device from pocket -speaks into it*) Goddot? Come in Goddot. Mission was a success. The Earthlings actually believed they were responsible for the termination of the human labeled Pepper. They were all taken away to a containment area called jail. It will be years before their memories return. I'll give you all the details when I get back. Klaatu. Yani. Enya. Over and out. (*looks around -exits*)

End

Suggested Props

steamer trunk

Broom- for Mac

toothpick- Mac

clipboards (w/ledger)-for Sam and Ella

small notebooks/pencil -cops and agents

donuts- Badham & Goodman

extra large coffee cup-Badham & Goodman

cocktail tray- Trixie

cigarette holder- Madame DuBoyse

martini glass- Madame DuBoyse

martini shaker- Noel

cell phones (2)- Agents Muledeer & Sullen

microphone (*not necessarily rea*l) - Edie Buffet

Production Notes

Remains To Be Seen was first presented at The White House Banquet Hall in St. Louis, Missouri in March, 1998. It was produced by Affton CenterStage.

The original venue at which Remains to Be Scene was first produced, afforded the production an actual "stage" in which the various scenes were centered; i.e. the Truck Rental offices, the home of Madame DuBoys, the police station. Other scenes such as the tavern scene with Iggy was played in the back of the room. Many of the scenes between Goodman and Badham were done among the tables of the audience. In essence the whole room was used.

A stage is not necessary for your production. But having a centralized point for the Rental Offices is a good idea.

There was no actual 'set' used. The only item was the "trunk". The trunk of course acted as the truck in the first scene, and then became a table or counter for the first rental office and second by standing it on end. It became another 'table' in the Madame DuBoys scene by placing a table cloth over it.

Made in the USA
San Bernardino, CA
06 January 2016